The Fifties

The Fifties

Photographs by the
Daily Mail

Gareth Thomas

This is a Parragon Book
First published in 2003

Parragon
Queen Street House
4 Queen Street
Bath, BA1 1HE, UK

Text © Parragon
All photographs © Associated Newspapers Archive
except jacket image of Elvis Presley reproduced courtesy of Corbis

Produced by Atlantic Publishing

A catalogue record for this book is available from the British Library.
ISBN 0 75259 025 1
Printed in China

The Fifties

The Fifties were a watershed in 20th-century history. As the decade began, food rationing was as bad as it was in 1945, and the threat of nuclear war was ever-present. Then rock and roll and Teddy Boys hit the streets, the word 'teenager' entered the vocabulary, and people became better off as the world economy was influenced by the prosperity of America.

Things began to move on all fronts. Television took over from radio and the status of celebrity had a new medium for growth. There were new stars: from Marilyn Monroe and Frank Sinatra to Brigitte Bardot and James Dean. Bill Haley rocked around the clock and even under the spectre of the Cold War and the Suez crisis Prime Minister Harold Macmillan would still claim 'you've never had it so good'.

The photographs in this book, from the archives of the Daily Mail, provide an impressionistic collage of life at a time when everything was 'All shook up'.

The Fifties

Sinatra's London debut is a sell-out

Above: Frank Sinatra at the London Palladium, having battled his way through a horde of teenage fans in advance of a performance. Sinatra was among the first singers to inspire such hysteria amongst teenagers, having established a youthful following during the 1940s with a more upbeat repertoire.

Opposite: Marlene Dietrich, the legendary German film star of the 1940s, who went on to become a cabaret singer in clubs around the world in the 1950s.

General Election 1950

Opposite: A female worker displays new Conservative Party posters at Central Office, Westminster, in preparation for the forthcoming general election. One of the posters clearly plays on the public fear of Communism, which, while more pronounced in the US, was intensified in Britain as a number of high-profile spying cases came to light.
Above: Members of the British Liberal Party prepare posters and leaflets for the general election at their St Pancras headquarters.

Labour wins election but majority cut

Above: Diners at the Savoy Hotel waiting to see election results: Clement Attlee had been elected Labour Prime Minister after the Second World War, with a landslide victory: although Churchill had been the great war hero, Labour appealed more now with Attlee's promise to win the peace. The party had great success initially, making major changes to the country, but by 1950 Labour was in disarray, with a much reduced majority and internal disputes.

Opposite: Labour leaders (l-r) Harold Wilson, Tom Williams, R. Southern and Aneurin Bevan.

The National Health Service

Opposite below: Aneurin Bevan on the steps of the Grand Hotel, London. Bevan was the Labour politician responsible for the formation of Britain's National Health Service. His resignation from the Cabinet in 1951 was to lead to much internal torment and contribute to Labour's losing the general election that year.

Opposite above: Election fever at Downing Street.

Above: The Queen was an immensely popular figure in Britain in the early 1950s.

The Festival of Britain, 1951

The Festival of Britain heralded the rebuilding of a heavily bombed site on London's South Bank. While looking back to the Great Exhibition of 1851, it looked forward too, to the hope of a brighter future for Britain now that WWII was over. One of the organisers, Gerald Barry, described the festival as 'a tonic to the nation'.

An aerial view of the festival site *(above)* showing the specially created, 365-foot diameter Dome of Discovery and the Skylon tower.

Opposite: the view from across the Thames and a section of the huge crowds in attendance.

Hard to Stomach

Despite the promise of fun and excitement offered by the festival, not everyone was won over by the idea. Earlier in the year provincial housewives protested in Westminster over rationing which still remained in place. Two women *(above)* hold aloft their 8d meat ration and carry placards which suggest that for many of those who were finding times hard, government spending of £11 million on the Festival of Britain was simply frivolous.

Opposite: A small crowd looks on as a group of boys play a game of roller-hockey in a London street, some of whom, it seems, brandish improvised hockey sticks. Although youth culture was to flourish in the 1950s, in the somewhat austere post-war years, and before the mass appeal of television took hold, children were to find many such ways of making their own entertainment.

The Dogs of War

Having failed to unite Korea at the end of World War II, Russian and US forces had occupied the southern half of the country until 1949. An invasion from the Communist north followed their withdrawal, which was soon to be joined by Chinese forces. This prompted United Nations troops to move in, in the autumn of 1950. In 1951, after failed armistice talks with Korea (which Russia refused to attend due to the UN's refusal to recognise Communist China) a US-led 'peace-keeping' force stepped up the offensive.

Above: A unit of the 26th Infantry Scout Dog Platoon on patrol in Korea.

Opposite: A Royal Day at the Races – the Queen, accompanied by Princesses Margaret and Elizabeth, the Earl of Rosebery, the Marquis of Blandford and behind them the Duchess of Kent, at the Epsom Derby.

Korea

Opposite: United Nations troops shield their ears from the deafening sounds of mortar and heavy machine-gun fire which they unleash on North Korean positions.

Opposite below: American troops assault North Korean positions beyond the 38th Parallel with heavy shelling from 155mm self-propelled guns.

Above: 'Little Joe', an adopted South Korean war orphan, with a corporal of the American 25th Infantry. 'Joe', in miniature uniform, shows off a captured weapon.

Sporting Greats

On July 10, 1951, Randolph Turpin of Great Britain defeated Sugar Ray Robinson of the USA on points, to win the Middleweight Championship of the World. They would fight again in September, however, when Turpin was to be knocked out in the 10th round.

Opposite: An exhausted, but elated Roger Bannister, having just broken the Championship record for the mile with a time of 4 minutes 7.8 seconds at White City. The dream of running a mile in under four minutes remained elusive, but he was to achieve this in 1954.

Radio v Television

Only 350,000 people had televisions in 1950 and, at least partly due to restricted hours and output, the status of television remained at first fairly low. In fact, it was often regarded as a trivial medium. Radio, on the other hand, was well established and regarded, and yet could frequently be avant-garde – for example, broadcasting plays by Samuel Beckett, Harold Pinter and Dylan Thomas. The incredible success of *The Goon Show*, though, was still something of a surprise, relying as it did on a high level of surrealism and anarchy for its humour. Launched in 1951 as *Crazy People*, perhaps much of its appeal lay in its knowing mockery of establishment types and its gratification of the British undercurrent of eccentricity. (*l-r above*: Peter Sellers, Harry Secombe and Spike Milligan) *Opposite*: The BBC Gramophone Library.

The King is Dead

Crowds lined the streets of Westminster to attend the funeral of King George VI, who passed away on February 6, 1952, aged 56. There was a genuine sense of loss for a monarch who had been widely regarded with affection.

Opposite above: The funeral procession on Horse Guards Parade.

Opposite below: The King lying in state in Westminster Hall.

Above: Prime Minister Winston Churchill arriving for the Accession Council, following the death of the King, to proclaim the accession of Princess Elizabeth as the new Queen.

Election address in India

India had been partitioned in 1947 and, although the country regarded itself as independent, remained a British dominion. Pandit Nehru, as the leader of the Congress Party, had been appointed Prime Minister of India, but Britain continued to have a hand in India's affairs as disputes still flared with Pakistan. 1952 was to see the first independent national election in India and here (*above*) vast crowds in Calcutta listen to a speech by Nehru.

Opposite: A fur-clad woman sits behind the wheel of a new Ford Consul which features a steering-column-mounted dashboard. However, although American industry was enjoying a period of prosperity, these remained hard times for most of the British population.

Simple pleasures

Above: Children's television programmes were to begin in earnest in the early 1950s. Here boys take part in the British Conker Championship at the BBC's Lime Grove Studios for a television broadcast.

Opposite: These youngsters play in the Thames at Tower Bridge as London experiences an early heatwave, with temperatures approaching 80° F in May 1952.

Atom Bomb Testing in Nevada

In 1950 US President Truman gave the go-ahead to a research programme into the hydrogen bomb, despite the fact that the General Advisory Committee on Atomic Energy had unanimously advised against pursuing such a programme, mainly on ethical grounds. But Truman became convinced of the need after the arrest in Britain in 1950 of Klaus Fuchs from the Atomic Energy Authority. Fuchs revealed at his trial that he had told Russian scientists everything he knew. The US therefore feared that Russia was rapidly developing superior weapons and by 1952 the US were testing thermo-nuclear devices in the Marshall Islands and Nevada Desert.

Opposite: At Yucca Flat, Nevada, marines emerge from their bunkers to witness the mushroom cloud produced by one such test.

Above: Stirling Moss helps out with the maintenance of his British-engineered ERA prior to the British Grand Prix at Silverstone. Moss came to be considered as the greatest driver never to win the world crown.

Everest conquered

The 1950s would prove to be a decade of exploration in many ways, as scientific discovery and technical advances heralded transformations in areas such as transportation and communications. However, it was exploration of a more geographical nature which captured the public imagination when the summit of Mount Everest was conquered for the first time – and by a British-led expedition. Tenzing Norgay Sherpa (*opposite*) and Edmund Hillary (*above*) were the two climbers to reach the summit, on 29 May 1953. The two were said to have reached the summit at the same time, although Hillary, a New Zealander, later claimed that he had been first to the top.

Sporting moments

Despite continued political turmoil around the world, people were able to relax a little more as
various rations were ended, allowing them a little more money for entertainments such as
attending sporting events. They were encouraged to see it as their duty to have some fun.
Above: Miss Maureen Connolly of the USA competes in the semi-final of the Ladies Singles
Championship at Wimbledon.
Opposite above: The Everest expedition party arrive at London Airport. Colonel Hunt holds an ice
pick aloft: to his left is Sherpa Tenzing, to his right, Edmund Hillary.
Opposite below: Colonel Hunt and his party attended a reception hosted by the New Zealand High
Commissioner. Edmund Hillary is greeted by Clement Attlee.

Coronation Street

The view from Buckingham Palace of the illuminations in The Mall to celebrate the Queen's Coronation on June 2, 1953. It was the first time that TV cameras had been allowed into Westminster Abbey and streets around the country were deserted as more than 20 million viewers were hooked to the screen.

Opposite: Streets all over Britain were decorated for the Coronation.

Royal Air Force salutes the crowned Queen

After the Coronation ceremony a formal procession took the family back to Buckingham Palace. In the evening they appeared on the balcony to wave to the vast cheering crowd below and to watch the Royal Air Force flypast salute. Prince Charles and Princess Anne were fascinated by the proceedings.

Hollywood dreams

Much of the optimism and dreams of affluence proved difficult for the British public to realise in the early 1950s. The consumer boom in the US filtered through, but these were difficult and disorientating times. Hollywood cinema provided a degree of escapism from the drudgery of day-to-day living and also presented new images of femininity and overt sexuality, which, whilst falling short of engendering a sexual revolution, certainly began to suggest new possibilities and roles for women. Brigitte Bardot, seen here with actor Kirk Douglas, first seduced the cameras and the public in 1953 at the Cannes Film Festival.

Opposite: The England international football team as they appeared in a friendly match against the Rest of Europe at Wembley on October 21, when they drew 4-4. Alf Ramsey is second from the left in the back row, and Stanley Matthews is on the far left of the front row.

Dancehall culture

Popular music and dancing provided yet another form of escapism in the 1950s and high-energy
styles such as the Jitterbug and Jive, introduced at first by black GIs during World War II, were
reaching mass audiences by 1953. Large-scale West Indian immigration began in the early 1950s with
an official inflow of around 12,000 people per year. However, although black music was embraced,
the immigrant population and their dancehalls were generally, and – through discrimination –
forcibly self-contained.

Fun and Games

Opposite: Jigsaw puzzles were introduced at Nunhead library as an experiment and proved so popular that the local council decided to extend the scheme across all of its libraries.
Above: Children playing a game of Ludo.

Designs for life

The family unit regained its importance in the Fifties, and women who had worked and experienced both the hardships and camaraderie of wartime returned to homemaking and motherhood, with the home itself becoming the central focus. For as the silver screen displayed images of Marilyn Monroe and Brigitte Bardot as sexually liberated women confronting men on their own terms, housewives were also being targeted by adverts for new fashions and labour-saving technologies in the colourful spirit and styles first presented at the Festival of Britain.

Ideal living

Above: The annual Ideal Home Exhibition held at Earls Court Olympia was an important arbiter of taste, bringing new designs and gadgets to the public attention. Shown here is the modern sitting room which now had to accommodate the television set.

Opposite: At the Ideal Home Exhibition, Princess Margaret watches a demonstration of a device which removes the pips from citrus fruit.

Ban the Bomb

Following the trial of Klaus Fuchs in 1950 for supplying atomic secrets to Russia, the US Congress insisted that no more sensitive knowledge be shared with Britain. By 1953, however,
Britain was testing H-bombs in the remote Australian outback; then in 1954 the US detonated a 15-megaton device on Bikini Atoll as they stepped up their programme in accordance with a belief in the deterrent effect of 'massive retaliatory power'.

Above: Protesters demonstrate against the bomb on the streets of London and invite MPs to join them.

Opposite: Lester Piggott after winning the Epsom Derby riding Never Say Die. It was his first of nine victories in the event.

Sports Personality of the Year

In 1954 Roger Bannister was to run the first sub-four-minute mile, for which he was awarded Sports Personality of the Year. Fellow runner Chris Chataway won the *Sportsview* trophy, awarded by the BBC's programme of the same name. The televised ceremony took place at the Savoy Hotel in London.

Opposite above: The England football squad return to London following a humiliating 7-1 defeat away to Hungary.

Opposite below: The incomparable Fangio chats with his long-term partner Donna Andreina in 1954. By 1957 Fangio had won the Formula One championship five times.

Hancock's Half Hour

Perhaps the first true sitcom, *Hancock's Half Hour*, written by Ray Galton and Alan Simpson, began on radio in 1954 and was to become something of a national institution. Rehearsing for the programme (*l-r*): Tony Hancock, Moira Lister, Bill Kerr and Sid James.

Opposite: Sophia Loren and Marlon Brando at a cinema in Rome. Brando had recently received an award for *On The Waterfront* and 1954 would also see the release of *The Wild One* in which he starred as a violent biker. The film had been adapted from a true story of American gang violence but predated the phenomenon of the Hell's Angels by several years. Youth subcultures were emerging in the Fifties though, on both sides of the Atlantic, and were frequently cited as disaffected movements, with a distrust of adults and sometimes a penchant for violence.

Teddy Boys

In Britain in the early Fifties, the first Teddy Boys emerged; working-class boys adopting a vaguely Edwardian style and frequently exhibiting anti-social behaviour - fighting and causing vandalism in the streets and dancehalls.

Above: A group of young Teds at a 'Best Dressed Teddy Boy Competition' in Nottingham.
Opposite: A competition winner receives the gift of the very latest in vacuum cleaners.

Cabinet of the Future?

Opposite: Some designs for the home were beginning to become less fussy, with cleaner lines and somewhat less decoration, perhaps as a backlash against the prevailing 'festival style'. The influence of the European modernists was becoming more evident in furniture design and architecture, and a radical display at the Ideal Home Exhibition looked even further forward, to the 'house of the future' (*opposite above left*).

Above: A policeman looks into the eyes of Anthony Eden, who was leading the Conservatives to their next election victory in 1955. Unlike Churchill, the great wartime leader, Eden campaigned on a peace ticket.

Churchill's Cabinet

Above: Winston Churchill and his Cabinet prior to the 1955 general election. Churchill had been re-elected in the 1951 election, which the Labour party had called in a disastrously unsuccessful attempt to strengthen their majority. In 1955 there was another election, with Anthony Eden standing for the Conservatives against Clement Attlee for Labour.

Election fever

Preparations for the 1955 general election at the mailroom at Conservative Party central office.
A woman prepares leaflets for national distribution under the watchful eye of Churchill's portrait.
Opposite: A huge, six by ten foot poster of Clement Attlee. Some claimed that in the absence of any
real policies, Attlee opted for 'cult of personality' tactics.

The Votes Are In

Crowds gather in Piccadilly Circus to hear the results of the 1955 election, which took place in May. Anthony Eden was to succeed Churchill as Prime Minister.

Opposite: Undisputed, undefeated, Heavyweight Champion of the World: on May 16 1955, Don Cockell of Britain took on Rocky Marciano of the US for the World Heavyweight Championship title. The fight was stopped in the 9th round, and Marciano remained undefeated. In fact, Rocky Marciano was to be the only undefeated heavyweight champion ever, winning all 49 of his fights, 43 by knockout.

Gentlemen Prefer Blondes?

Marilyn Monroe had come to the attention of the public as an actress in the early 1950s, and although some felt that she was limited in terms of her acting abilities, she was to become Hollywood's most famous female sex symbol. The publication of the Kinsey Report on female sexual behaviour in 1953 was instrumental in breaking various sexual taboos and within just a few years, the boundaries of acceptable sexual explicitness had broadened considerably. Hollywood in particular began to present a new, blonde, busty, idealised image of women.

Opposite: Britain's answer to the well endowed platinum blonde came in the form of Diana Dors, and although her celebrity was initially manufactured, she would later prove herself as an actress. Seen here at 'The Night of 100 Stars' at the London Palladium, with comedian Jimmy Edwards.
Above: Marilyn Monroe in a famous scene from *The Seven Year Itch*.

Image Problem

Opposite: Three 18-year-old English Teddy Boys working as stewards on a cruiseship are prompted to visit the Wellington *Evening Post* in New Zealand, to defend their image, in response to an article the paper had published on Teddy Boys carrying knives.

Above: Pianist and showman Liberace (right), with his mother and brother, George.

Young Lives Cut Short

The last woman to be hanged in Britain, Ruth Ellis, was sent to the gallows on July 13, 1955. 28-year-old Ruth had shot and killed her lover David Blakely following a miscarriage which, it emerged in court, she had suffered ten days after Blakely had beaten her up. The press had been largely sympathetic to her case, but despite mitigating circumstances, there would be no respite for Ruth. It has been suggested that although she showed remorse for her crime, and was not thought to be a danger to the public, Ruth Ellis was regarded as a woman of dubious sexual morality, and perhaps it was this, rather than her actual crime, that finally condemned her.

Opposite: Ruth's parents visit their daughter in jail.

Above: John Neville, Michael Benthall and Richard Burton enjoy a break from their rehearsals of *Othello* which Benthall was directing. The previous year Burton had narrated Dylan Thomas's *Under Milk Wood*, which Thomas had taken years to supply to Douglas Cleverdon at the BBC and which Thomas had almost lost before leaving for America where he would die in 1953.

Death of a Young Rebel, and the Birth of a Legend

James Dean was to star in only three films in his short life, but through the characters he portrayed, and in his off-stage persona, Dean was to convey the spirit of alienated youth, rejected by the adult world and searching for a way out in speed and excitement. Within two weeks of Dean's death behind the wheel of a sports car at the age of 24, *Rebel Without A Cause* was released and Dean's status as a legend, at least amongst his contemporaries, was assured.

Above: James Dean's grave in his hometown of Fairmount, Indiana.

Fifties icon

Marilyn Monroe, the quintessential icon of the fifties, with her third husband playwright Arthur Miller, who once said of her, 'With all her radiance she was surrounded by a darkness'. In 1959 she starred alongside Jack Lemmon and Tony Curtis in Billy Wilder's *Some Like It Hot,* which became a milestone of film comedy.

Affluence at home

Britain was to become more affluent in the latter half of the Fifties, with more people able to afford such things as domestic appliances and stylish home furnishings. As purchasing power increased, so did the desire for conspicuous consumption, bolstered by rapidly developing and innovative technologies and the lifestyles which were sold with them.

Above: A new electric cooker, the 'Super Comet', which featured an automatic timer.

A Loss of Innocence

Children were still very much expected to be seen and not heard in 1956, but teenagers were finding a voice of their own and beginning to express it loudly. When rock and roll exploded onto the scene in the mid-Fifties, it was just the catalyst that the youth required to consolidate their anti-adult, anti-authority stance. 'Rock Around The Clock' by Bill Haley and his Comets was first heard during the opening titles of the film *The Blackboard Jungle* in 1955, and topped the charts for five months.

Above: Youngsters in Glasgow play a game of marbles in the street.

By 1956 *Rock Around The Clock* was the title of a film, featuring Bill Haley and his Comets, and was not only causing disturbances at the theatres where it was shown, with seats being ripped out of the stalls, but was disturbing many adults who regarded the music as debased and the behaviour it provoked as deeply troubling. The press blamed poor discipline, moral decline, and the education system, some press articles even going as far as to refer to youth armies in Egypt and Nazi Germany as examples of young people out of control.

Opposite: Teenage Teddy Boys by a cinema showing *Rock Around The Clock*. Police doused the crowd inside with fire hoses as they vandalised the theatre.

Rock and Roll

Despite initial outrage, the energy and excitement of rock and roll rapidly attracted a huge following throughout the younger elements in Britain.

Above: Tony Crombie and his Rock and Roll Rockets rehearse for *Saturday Night At The Palladium* a programme to be broadcast on the year-old commercial television station ITV.

Opposite: Britain's 'Prince of Rock and Roll' Tommy Steele, who came to fame at the age of 19, forming his own group called The Cavemen in 1956.

The Suez Crisis, 1956

The British Government had long regarded the Suez Canal as a lifeline of its Empire, and when the Egyptian King Farouk, over whom the British held sway, was removed by the Egyptian army a crisis erupted. There was talk of evacuating British troops, but the fear was that Britain would subsequently lose its grip on the Middle East and Africa, and after an initial withdrawal and some political manoeuvring, an Anglo-French force supported by Israel, launched an attack on the Egyptian army. Britain then ignored calls from the UN to withdraw, and although initial attacks appeared effective, soon the Suez Canal was blocked, and Middle Eastern oil ceased to flow.

Opposite above: A ship passing down the Suez Canal.

Opposite below: A protest over Eden's handling of the Suez crisis by the 'British Peace Committee'.

Above: Back on the home front: a debutantes' rock and roll ball.

War-torn Budapest

When, at the 20th Congress of the Communist Party, Chairman Khrushchev was to denounce Stalin, many of the East European countries under Soviet control and suppressed by the Stalinist regime were thrown into turmoil. Following uprisings in East Germany and Poland the USSR drew the line with Hungary, which – in 1956 – was in violent revolt: the police and military had joined forces with the people, who were out on the streets en masse. The secret police were being hunted down and executed in the streets and, when the Hungarian leader announced that Hungary would withdraw from the Warsaw Pact, Russia sent tanks into Budapest. They were ruthless and in just three days of fighting, up to 30,000 people were killed. Britain and the US offered moral support and condemned Russia, but did nothing more, being taken up with the Suez Crisis.

Opposite above: A Russian tank in the heart of war-torn Budapest.
Opposite below: A female Hungarian freedom fighter during a temporary ceasefire.
Above: Hungarians in London march on Downing Street to appeal for intervention.

The kids join the craze

Although rock and roll had not long previously been demonised as a corrupter of youth, there is little evidence of it to be found in this photograph. During the school holidays, this school hall was open at Lena Gardens School in Hammersmith for music and dancing to entertain the children. They danced to rock and roll, jive and more traditional songs, performed at the piano by one of their teachers.

Opposite: After the Hungarian rebel leader was promised safe passage if he left of his own accord, Imre Nagy was captured and executed and a government was put in place by Russia. Thousands of refugees continued to attempt escape into Austria across inhospitable marshlands, but the borders were heavily patrolled by Russian troops who forced women and children back at gunpoint, and took some of the men away, never to be seen again.

Testing the H-Bomb

As the US and Russia continued to develop nuclear weapons, the British felt compelled to do the same, believing that even if they were to be attacked with conventional weapons, they would have to strike back with an H-Bomb to demonstrate that Britain could and would strike decisively at any nation who posed a threat. Although it was designed to act as a deterrent, such a policy was symptomatic of, and indeed added to, the paranoia of the times.

Opposite and above: Engineers of the British armed forces prepare for H-Bomb tests on Christmas Island in the Pacific Ocean.

Busby Babes defeated by Villa

Above: Duncan Edwards of Manchester United and England as England play Scotland at Wembley. United's 'Busby Babes' were defeated 2-1 in the FA Cup at Wembley in 1957 by Aston Villa. Villa captain Johnny Dixon (*opposite*) holds the Cup aloft, supported by his team.

Fifties women

Women of the Fifties were in a particularly contradictory position. They were homemakers who had proved themselves in wartime, but were now discouraged from pursuing careers, and they were sexually awakened, but objectified as sex symbols. Even this objectification could be seen as empowering though, for women, taking their lead from Bardot and Monroe, and backed up by the independence that they had demonstrated in the war years, were acutely aware of the power they could hold over men, and showed that their attitude towards sex could be positioned on a more equal footing. The Fifties also saw the launch of the Miss World beauty contests (*above*).

The entertainers

Opposite above: The Beverley Sisters, wrapped up warm with ear-muffs and lion-crested coats, return from a trip to the US during which they were to have their first hit record there with 'Greensleeves'.

Opposite below: Ingrid Bergman and Cary Grant visit the Royal Opera House, Covent Garden, where they meet Margaret Lee and Brenda Bolton of the Royal Ballet who are appearing in *Indiscreet*, a Stanley Donen film being made there.

Above: British comedic actor Norman Wisdom with Swedish actressr Anita Ekberg, the star of European films such as *La Dolce Vita*.

Frank and Lauren

Frank Sinatra, who by now had established himself as a movie star as well as a singer, with Lauren Bacall, the widow of Humphrey Bogart who had died the year before. Rumours were to abound that the couple were to wed.

Opposite: Bengali refugees flock to Calcutta after fleeing a camp in Bihar, having been led to believe that they would be rehabilitated in their own province of West Bengal. They were originally Hindu refugees who faced persecution in the mainly Islamic Pakistan. The Indian Government refused to help these people unless they returned to Bihar. However, many were ill and claimed that they were neglected there, preferring to take their chances on the streets of Calcutta.

Trams on the road

Above: Cobblestones and tram cars: but crossing the road was much less hazardous in the Fifties. This view is from Blackfriars Bridge in London in 1959.

Opposite: A Ferta unit of the Algerian Rebel Army, consisting of around 30 men led by a lieutenant. In 1954 Algeria had rebelled against the French, who regarded the African nation as part of their own country: this was to lead to a long and bloody war. By 1958, generals of the French army, believing that their government was about to negotiate a settlement with the Algerian FLN rebels, threatened to seize power in France, bringing the country to the brink of civil war. The French then approved the recall of Charles De Gaulle, who began the long process of negotiations which would ultimately grant Algeria independence.

The Emergence of the CND Movement.

Towards the end of 1957, J. B. Priestley had published an article in the *New Statesman* entitled 'Britain and the Nuclear Bomb', in which he expressed the view that Britain might set a moral example to the world by abandoning its H-Bomb programme. The article received a huge amount of support, from well known clerics, writers, artists and other public figures, as well as from the general public themselves, and the CND was really formed out of the discussions which Priestley had triggered. Some 5000 people attended the first meeting at Central Hall, Westminster, and then on April 6, following a demonstration in London's Trafalgar Square, hundreds of people, swelling to thousands, marched in protest to the atomic research facility at Aldermaston in Berkshire.

The Empire Games

Above: Chris Chataway, Peter Driver and Roger Bannister embark on the first leg of a relay from Buckingham Palace, carrying a silver baton which contains a message from the Queen to be read by the Duke of Edinburgh at the opening of The Empire Games in Cardiff.

Opposite: US Vice-President Nixon pays a visit to Britain in November, meeting up with the former Prime Minister Winston Churchill. The same month, Nixon's wife holds a press conference for women (*below*).

Phoenix from the Flames

Opposite: Bobby Charlton of Manchester United trains in his FA Cup shirt which bears the emblem of a phoenix, symbolising the resurgence of Manchester United following the Munich air crash on February 6, 1958, in which eight of the team's players were killed.

Above: The wreckage of the BEA Elizabethan Airliner, in which a total of twenty-three people died.

Sir Matt still 'undefeated'

Above: Sir Matt Busby reading a book perhaps fittingly titled *The Undefeated*. In May 1958, just three months after the Munich disaster, Manchester United lost the FA Cup Final 2-0 to Bolton Wanderers.

Opposite: Signs are unveiled for Britain's first stretch of motorway, to be opened by the Prime Minister, Harold Macmillan, who had succeeded Anthony Eden the previous year. Macmillan called the eight-mile Preston bypass in Lancashire 'the symbol of the opening of a new era of motor travel in the United Kingdom'.

Aldermaston to London

Above: 1959 was to witness the second CND march, this time reversing the route of the previous year, travelling from Aldermaston to London for a rally in Trafalgar Square. The march was led by John Collins, the Canon of St Paul's, and Sir Richard Acland.

Opposite: In December, anti-nuclear protesters take their first direct action, clashing with police, labourers and airforce men at a US rocket base in Swaffham, Norfolk. Protesters from the 'Direct Action Committee Against Nuclear War' breached security at the base to surround machinery being used to build launching sites, but were eventually all removed.

Protests in London

The CND protesters were not the only demonstrators to March through London in 1959. Members of the 'Coloured Peoples Progressive Association' display their placards in Whitehall (*opposite*) after the murder of Kelso Cochrane in Notting Hill by supporters of Oswald Mosley. The previous year race riots had flared in Notting Hill for several days, after Teddy Boys, fired up by right-wing racist groups, began attacking black people indiscriminately.

Above: The Aldermaston to London march.

Windsor Castle 1959

Quiet moments for the Queen and Prince Philip at Windsor Castle in 1959. Sugar the Queen's corgi accompanied them throughout the photo call. In June, the Queen began an extensive tour of Canada and the United States. She had just discovered that she was pregnant again, but carried on, determined to carry out her plans. A romance had begun between Princess Margaret and Antony Armstrong-Jones, which was to lead to their marriage the following year.

Opposite: Billy Wright leads England on to the field before defeating Scotland 1-0. Bobby Charlton put in a sublime performance and scored the goal.

Never Had it so Good?

With the lifting of restrictions on hire purchase in 1958 came a massive consumer boom. People who could previously not afford refrigerators or cars now found that with a small downpayment, they could. But whilst this, and the boom in foreign travel that came with the advent of package holidays, provided the illusion of prosperity, compared to much of Europe Britain's productivity was slower, its exports smaller and inflation higher.

Above: The first Morris Mini-Minor, known as the Mini, also sold as the Austin 7.

Opposite: Two new designs of the Ford Anglia, which was targeted at just about everyone, advertised as a sporty, stylish, economical family car.

Leading women

Above: Brigitte Bardot arriving in London to film *Babette Goes to War*.
Opposite above: Prince Rainier and Princess Grace of Monaco window-shopping in London's Burlington Arcade.
Opposite below: Barbara Castle speaking at the Labour Party Conference in Blackpool.

The master film-maker

Opposite: Alfred Hitchcock was prolific in his film-making throughout the Fifties, and was referred to as the Master. Hitchcock invariably played bit parts in his movies as a trademark. Here he plays a passing pedestrian in *I Confess*.

Above: Film star Rita Hayworth and her husband James Hill fly to Berlin from London Airport.

Hancock the rebel

Opposite: Tony Hancock making his film debut in *The Rebel*, which tells the story of a city clerk rebelling against the dull routine of his life, in the tradition of anti-establishment films and literature which emerged in the Fifties.
Above: Humphrey Lyttelton and his band play with the London Jazz Club on the banks of the Thames following a boat trip.

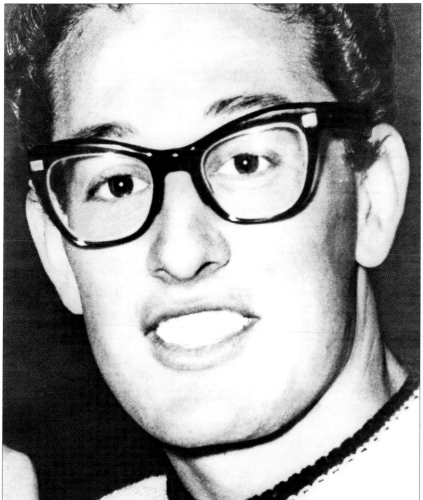

The Day the Music Died

Above: Rock and roll had begun to tail off towards the end of the 1950s. A further blow was dealt in 1959, when Buddy Holly and the Big Bopper were killed in a plane crash on their way to a performance.
Opposite: Smartly dressed lads at an Essex dancehall.

ACKNOWLEDGEMENTS

The photographs in this book are from the archives of the *Daily Mail*.
Particular thanks to Steve Torrington, Dave Sheppard, Brian Jackson, Alan Pinnock,
Richard Jones and all the staff.

Thanks also to Cliff Salter, Richard Betts, Gareth Thomas
Peter Wright, Trevor Bunting and Simon Taylor.
Design by John Dunne.